RICH HABITS

THE DAILY SUCCESS HABITS OF WEALTHY INDIVIDUALS

FIND OUT HOW THE RICH GET SO RICH
(THE SECRETS TO FINANCIAL
SUCCESS REVEALED)

T0182451

RICH HABITS

THE DAILY SUCCESS HABITS OF WEALTHY INDIVIDUALS

FIND OUT HOW THE RICH GET SO RICH (THE SECRETS TO FINANCIAL SUCCESS REVEALED)

Thomas C. Corley CPA, CFP, M.S. Tax

Copyright © 2009 by Thomas C. Corley.

Langdon Street Press
212 3rd Avenue North, Suite 290
Minneapolis, MN 55401
612.455.2293
www.langdonstreetpress.com

To order a copy of this book go to: www.richhabits.net

All rights reserved. No part of this publication may be reproduced, stored in a retrieval system, or transmitted, in any form or by any means, electronic, mechanical, photocopying, recording, or otherwise, without the prior written permission of the author.

ISBN - 978-1-934938-93-5
ISBN - 1-934938-93-9
LCCN - 2009942792

Typeset by James Arneson

Printed in the United States of America

TABLE OF CONTENTS

INTRODUCTION

The fact is: success is elusive. Why? Why are the rich so rich? Only about five percent of the population in the United States realizes true financial success. What traits do they possess that make them so successful? Few ever find out. Unfortunately, *how to be financially successful in life* is not a subject that is taught in our schools. We are all in the same boat, attempting through trial and error to figure it out on our own.

I have devoted years of researching the daily habits of wealthy people. I have incorporated what I have learned from my research into the "Rich Habits Program," which is designed to provide timely, easy-to-follow guidance on achieving unlimited personal and financial success. Wealth is not just a byproduct of random luck, education, hard work, or inheritance. Financial success is a foolproof process. Within these pages is the twenty first century blueprint for financial success!

I am a certified public accountant and certified financial planner to more than one thousand individuals and small businesses. The genesis of this book began when a struggling client came to my office seeking advice. The client's business was growing; however, he had difficulty in making ends meet, particularly at payroll time. In sheer desperation he asked, "What am I doing wrong?" For months I analyzed his business, his expenses, processes, labor rates, and industry comparative data. I even sought advice from a "rich" client in the same industry, with a similar level of gross revenues and whose business shared comparable demographics. Together we could find nothing that stood out, no glaring deficiency.

At a lunch meeting with my struggling client, some weeks later, I confessed that I could not diagnose the cause of my client's financial problems. The client was not happy. I was not happy. We sat in silence at our table for some time. In an effort to break the uncomfortable silence I asked my client what he did when he came home at night. There was an immediate shift in my client's demeanor. An almost impish look took hold and he asked me, "Which night?"

"Pick your favorite night," I suggested.

The client told me that would be Wednesday.

"What do you do on Wednesday nights?" I pressed the client.

The client leaned in, eyeing the restaurant and said ever so quietly, "I get a couple of ladies of the night, a few bottles of wine and…" The client, in response to my obvious look of shock, stopped mid-sentence. "I'm sorry," he said. "I should not have shared that with you. I talk way too much sometimes."

I assured him that I was an Irish Catholic New York boy from a family of eight and that there was very little I had not seen in my life. My shock was not from moral indignation, but from the realization that I had been asking my client all the wrong questions these past months. The epiphany I had was that there was much more to financial problems than meets the eye and that I needed to ask the right questions. I eventually came up with a twenty-question list that, over a five-year period, I asked to just about every rich or poor client I had, as well as every business partner or person I knew.

The data I gathered from these questions made me realize that there is a difference the size of the Grand Canyon in the way rich people and poor people live their daily lives. This one client unknowingly took me down a path toward the discovery of the secret to financial success.

The Insurance Salesman

"I just can't take it anymore," Phoenix Upman murmured into his half-empty pint glass. He ran his short, plump fingers through what little hair was left on his head as his cigarette burned out in the ashtray beside him.

"Bad day?" the bartender asked nonchalantly as he leaned over the bar, perusing the sports section. He didn't seem particularly interested, but pretended to be for his customer's sake.

Phoenix managed a sort of angry snort that gave way to forced, hollow laughter. "More like a bad life." He drained the rest of his beer and slid the empty mug forward for a refill. "Last night I had to tell my son that we could not afford to send him to college. We just don't have the money. We can't even swing tuition at Brookline."

Brookline, the local community college, gave discounted rates to county residents — practically giving away an education. The bartender sensed immediately how pathetic Phoenix's financial situation must be if he couldn't even afford Brookline. The bartender had managed to get himself through two years there with what little savings he had, supplemented by the tips from this place.

"Not even Brookline, huh?"

"No," Phoenix said. He lit up another cigarette and took a long, slow drag, letting his eyelids close as he held in his breath.

"This one is on me." The bartender set a fresh pint down in front of Phoenix and contemplated the troubled man. Although younger than the bartender, that was not obvious by looking at Phoenix. His receding hairline and expanding waistline made him look older, as did the deep crease between his eyes and the wrinkles snaked across his forehead. Nothing about him was particularly distinct. His shirtsleeves, rolled up to mid-forearm, had blotchy blue ink stains. "What do you do for a living?"

"I sell insurance," he said, too quickly perhaps. "What I mean is I try. What I make is barely enough to live on, let alone put away for something like college." Phoenix rolled a peanut between his thumb and forefinger, his gaze fixed somewhere across the bar. He sat for a long while, quiet, slowly rolling the peanut, unblinking. "How'd I get to be such a failure?" he murmured to himself.

The bartender returned to the article he was reading. Phoenix set the peanut down on the bar and wrapped his hand back around the cold glass, lifting the mug to his lips once again, draining his latest pint. "You know, even if I died there's not much. I don't even have enough insurance to make that worthwhile." He slid the glass forward, signaling another refill. "Some salesman I am," he muttered under his breath. He pinched the bridge of his nose and closed his eyes tight, scrunching up his face.

"You driving, man?" the bartender asked.

"I'm not far from here, just a few blocks. I'll be fine."

"I don't know; you've been here a while."

Phoenix glanced at the bartender, a pleading look in his eyes. He knew he had worn out his welcome, but how could he go home and face his son after last night? It was clear the bartender was going to cut him off. Sensing this, Phoenix laid out some cash and pushed back from the bar. Without saying a word, he shrugged into his coat and cap, pulling his cap down tight on his head before making his way down the length of the bar toward the exit.

Outside was dark and Phoenix could see his breath hanging in the air before him. There were no stars; they were lost somewhere behind opaque December clouds. He made his way over to his black subcompact and fumbled in his pockets for the keys. Inside the car was not much better; he could feel his fingers going numb from the cold. Phoenix lit one last cigarette and sat back, waiting for the engine to warm up.

He let his head roll back and sighed to himself something about bad luck. His eyelids fell shut as he took a long drag off the cigarette. The smoke swirled up and around his head in wispy grey ribbons before pooling in a thin cloud near the ceiling of the car. Phoenix opened his eyes and watched the trail of smoke dance away from the butt. He shook his head slowly. He thought about what he might say to his son, if the boy would even talk to him. A sudden knock on the driver-side window startled Phoenix.

"Jesus," he muttered, fumbling around on the floor for the still-burning cigarette that fell from his hand with the knock on the window. He found the cigarette and snubbed what was left in the overflowing ashtray before rolling down his window. "Can I help you?" he asked gruffly, staring up at the stranger who had interrupted his thoughts.

"I was just about to ask you the same thing."

"Excuse me?" Phoenix looked up at the stranger standing just outside the car. "Do I know you?"

"My name is Champ Dailey," the stranger said, sticking out a gloved hand. Phoenix reluctantly obliged, loosely gripping the soft, black leather, and quickly recoiled.

And your name is?" the stranger asked.

"Phoenix Upman."

"Hi, Mr. Upman. I couldn't help but overhear you back in the bar. I'm truly sorry for your troubles."

Phoenix wasn't quite sure what to make of this. When the bartender was pretending not to ignore Phoenix all he'd wanted was a little bit of sympathy, but now, coming from this stranger, well, it just made him feel more pathetic. Phoenix waved off the comment, shaking his head, and fixed his gaze straight ahead.

"I'd like you to come by my office on Monday," Champ continued. "I can help you." Champ pulled a business card from his pocket and extended the card. Phoenix took the card and studied it suspiciously.

"Help me? You don't even know me."

"You'd be surprised," Champ replied, a warm grin spreading across his face.

"What are you like a loan shark or something? I'm not getting involved in that, I got enough problems as it is," Phoenix said.

"No, Mr. Upman," Champ loosed a slow rolling laugh and continued, "just a man looking in a very old mirror." With that he turned to walk across the parking lot, calling over his shoulder, "Monday, twelve o'clock."

Phoenix's eyes followed Champ in the rearview mirror, watching as he got into his car and pulled out of the lot. After Champ had gone, Phoenix found himself staring at his own reflection. "Old mirror?" he repeated to himself as he studied his own face. He glanced down at the business card still in his hands. "Nothing to lose at this point, I suppose." He tucked the business card in his wallet and set off for home.

Phoenix was restless as he showered and dressed for work on Monday morning. He could think only of the strange encounter and his upcoming meeting with this Champ Dailey fellow. Phoenix had lost hope long ago, but on his lunch hour that day, as he walked up Broad Street towards the address on the card, his curiosity compelled him forward. As the numbers climbed, the buildings became much nicer, taller, and more ornate. Finally, at the corner of Broad and First, he came to a stop in front of the grandest building on the street. He grew dizzy as he looked straight up, taking in the façade of the building. Phoenix double-checked the address on the card to make sure he had the right place: 700 Broad Street. He sighed, futilely trying to count the number of floors from the street.

"May I help you?" the doorman said, interrupting his tally.

"I have a meeting with Champ Dailey."

"Yes, sir," the doorman replied, swinging open the tall glass door and welcoming Phoenix inside. "Take the left bank of elevators, the ones marked twenty to thirty-five. Mr. Dailey's office is on the twenty-first floor. Exit the elevator to your right."

Phoenix nodded, distracted by the lobby buzzing with energy. He found the right elevator and got in, his finger dancing over the button. He couldn't help but wonder what he was getting himself into.

The doors opened to an expansive reception area. Phoenix was immediately overwhelmed. The room was larger than the entire sales department back at his office. He hesitated before exiting the elevators, checking the floor number again just to make sure he was in the right place.

As he walked out of the elevator, Champ Dailey greeted him. "Mr. Upman, I'm so glad you came. Did you have much trouble finding the building?"

"Um…uh, no," Phoenix replied. "I hope, uh, this isn't a bad time or anything. I can come back later if you're busy. The place seems busy."

"No, I was expecting you, Mr. Upman. Please, follow me," Champ instructed, leading him past the reception area and through a short hallway. Phoenix was stunned when Champ swung the door open to reveal an opulent office. The wood floors and oak-lined walls warmed the cavernous room, and numerous paintings provided splashes of color. Phoenix took in the expansive room and conceded that this was the most impressive office he had ever been in.

Phoenix took a better look at Champ. He seemed taller then Phoenix remembered, and lean with a full head of silver-grey hair. His soft, blue eyes radiated a kind of welcoming warmth, which put Phoenix at ease, at least a little. The man had a kind of good-natured air about him, and he seemed casual and relaxed.

"I'm so glad you came," Champ said. He directed Phoenix to an empty chair in front of his desk.

"I'm sorry about the other night. I guess…I, um, I was just, you know…"

"No need to apologize," Champ broke in, nodding sympathetically. Champ sat, considering the man across from him for a moment. Phoenix shifted nervously in his chair as the silence settled between them. He couldn't help being distracted by his surroundings, peering around at the paintings and luxurious décor.

"I've been where you are, you know." Champ finally spoke, leaning in ever so slightly. "I've been in the pits of darkness and despair."

Phoenix looked confused as his eyes settled back on the man seated across the desk. "Despair? From the looks of things I'd say you are a continent from despair."

Champ paused, smirking just a bit. "I am, now; but not too long ago things were a mess. No hope, no direction, everything in life seemed to pass me by. I almost lost my family over my circumstances. I guess you could say I've come a long way." Champ closed his eyes and the smile faded from his face. "When I heard you the other night at the bar, it brought back a lot of painful memories."

Phoenix shifted again in his chair. He felt as though he were intruding on a private moment. Champ didn't seem to notice Phoenix. Phoenix cleared his throat, twice.

"Funny thing that I was in that bar that night. I'd never been to that bar before. After I left, I kept wondering why our paths had crossed that night. What put me in that particular bar on that particular night?" Champ seemed to drift again. "The only conclusion I could reach was that something intended I be there, meant me to be there, to meet you."

Phoenix stared at Champ, considering his words carefully. "Like what? Like fate, or something?"

"Fate, yes."

"Why? What's so important about me that fate would have us meet? Why me?"

A smile broke on Champ's face and he sat up straight, his eyes wide as if he had a long-kept secret he was ready to share. "I believe it was intended that I pull you out of this hole you're in. I am sure now that you are the very opportunity I was told about. Yes, I am certain that you represent my opportunity to return the favor that I received a lifetime ago when I was an altogether different man."

"I don't understand," Phoenix replied.

"You see, some years ago I was told that I might be called upon to help another in need. I was told I would know him when I saw him because I would see the mirror image of my old self. I didn't understand the meaning of this at the time, but then you came along and finally it all made sense. Listening to you the other night, I recognized immediately that you were the person I was meant to help."

"How did you know all this? How did you know to look for me?"

"Because he told me to," Champ said.

"Who?"

"My mentor, my advisor. In a lot of ways, the man who saved my life."

"Who?" Phoenix asked again.

"J.C. Jobs."

Champ went on to explain how J.C. Jobs was responsible for Champ's turn-around, and many others just like him.

"He enabled us to reach levels of success we had never dreamed possible." Phoenix listened intently, absorbing every word.

"I was given ten laws by J.C. Jobs. He called them the 'Rich Habits.' I was told to live these ten principles for thirty days and meet back with him. He promised me that if I followed these ten rules, my situation would improve. At that point, I had nothing to lose; so I did exactly as he instructed and met back up with him after the thirty days had passed." Champ paused and drew his shoulders back.

"And…?" Phoenix prompted.

"And the rest is history. What you see all around you here is the byproduct of living the Rich Habits every day. The Rich Habits completely transformed my life."

"And now you're going to share these principles with me?" Phoenix asked, a trace of excitement on his face and in his voice.

"No," Champ replied. He leaned back in his chair and crossed his legs, eyes focused squarely on Phoenix.

"What? Then why am I here?" Phoenix furrowed his brow and his eyes became narrow. A creeping suspicion that Champ had been wasting his time now took root, and Phoenix contemplated getting up right then and there and marching out of the cavernous office without so much as a glance back. Still something kept him anchored to his seat.

"The principles are just an overview of a more comprehensive process. J.C. has created a program he calls the Rich Habits Training Program. He and his team train individuals, such as you, in following the Rich Habits. My responsibility ends when I come across a candidate who meets J.C.'s mirror test." Champ reached across his expansive desk for a pen and scrawled a phone number on a sheet of paper.

"Here is the number where you can reach J.C.'s office. Call this number first thing tomorrow morning."

"And what do I say? How much does this training program cost?" Phoenix asked.

"There is no cost when you are sponsored, Mr. Upman. Just let J.C.'s office know that Champ Dailey sponsored you. They can help you, Mr. Upman. Of that, I am certain."

With that, Champ stood, smoothing his jacket and directed Phoenix to the door. Phoenix was slow to get up, reluctant to leave, as he clung to the piece of paper with

J.C.'s phone number. He couldn't help but think that the most valuable thing in the whole building was this simple scrap of paper now in his possession.

The next morning Phoenix did as Champ instructed. As soon as he got to work he called the number. A woman answered.

"Hello, my name is Phoenix Upman and I'm trying to reach J.C. Jobs. Champ Dailey told me to give him a call."

"What may I tell Mr. Jobs this is in reference to?" the woman asked. "Champ Dailey told me to say that I was sponsored by him."

"Certainly, Mr. Upman," the woman replied. She took down Phoenix's contact information and said she would relay the message to Mr. Jobs. Then she hung up the phone. Within a few minutes the same woman called Phoenix back with an appointment for the next Rich Habits training session.

The Secretary

"What am I going to do with her?" John Andrews, CEO of Sunblade, Inc., a distributor of saw blades in northern New Jersey, had just been informed by his office manager Nina, that Dee had called in for the third time this month to say she was going to be late. The mornings were important for Sunblade, especially Dee's role, which required an hour each morning calling both existing customers and prospects. It was a process the company put in place years ago, and when the process was applied consistently, sales were the result. Dee's absence meant no calls and lost sales for the week.

"John, you keep bending the rules for Dee and she just keeps pushing the envelope to see how much further you'll bend them. I told you last year to fire her. Why don't you just fire her already?" Nina had lost her patience for Dee's poor attendance and sense of entitlement. Nina wanted Dee fired but John just could not bring himself to do so.

"But I see so much potential in her, Nina. If I could just break her of some of these bad habits she holds on to, she would shine. I just know it."

Dee Worthy worked as a secretary for Sunblade. Her pay for the past two years was meager, primarily due to her "bad habits," as John began to call them. She was a young twenty-four-year-old, heavy set to the point of being unhealthy. She had a pleasant smile and an attractive face. Most of Dee's colleagues described her as a hardworking, conscientious, and a punctual employee. These same people also described Dee as lazy, neglectful, and tardy. At times she exhibited creativity, a great work ethic, and incredible promise, but eventually she always fell back into tardiness, distraction, and indifference. The root cause, many suspected, were family issues from which Dee sought refuge in food. Her near-obesity caused health issues, which manifested in frequent sick days.

"A vicious circle of bad habits," John admonished Dee at one of their many meetings following a cycle of absences.

In Dee's family circle she was the functional one. Her ability to earn even a meager income made her the family banker. John often tried to paint a picture of her reality, how her family was dragging her down due to their own bad habits and their seeming inability to draw a consistent income. Unfortunately, Dee never took John's advice to heart. John recognized her vulnerability when it came to her family. Recognizing this weakness, her family took full advantage of Dee. Dee's insecurities didn't help matters, either. "I'm not that smart," she often said to others around the office. "My cousin is the smart one in the family. She got the main course and all I got were the leftovers."

"Her cousin?" John barked at Nina. "The smart one with two children out of wedlock – who lives with her and hasn't had a job in over two years? Jeez."

"I need to talk to you about something personal."

John had grown so tired of these repetitive personal meetings with Dee, which were more and more frequent.

"I got a second job as a bartender and I will need to leave early on Fridays."

John could tell from the look on Dee's face that she feared these meetings as much as John had grown tired of them. "How early Dee?" he asked in a clearly frustrated tone.

"I need to leave at four p.m."

Work hours ended for everyone else at five-thirty p.m. John knew this would create a major problem for the other employees, who would resent seeing John as catering to Dee and bending the rules again, rules that didn't seem to apply to Dee. John feared that he would be sending the wrong message to everyone if he didn't exact some concessions from Dee.

"I will agree to this on two conditions."

"Yes?" Dee replied sheepishly.

"The first condition is that you will have to make up the missing time on Thursdays." Some members of the staff worked late on Thursdays, finalizing orders for the next week, so he felt her presence might thwart any staff assertions that Dee was getting special treatment.

"The second condition is that if you fail to live up to condition number one, by the third time I will have no choice but to terminate your employment."

Dee, very reluctantly, agreed to the terms. What choice did she have really? She needed the extra money. Dee left his office and as the day wore on she grew resentful of her boss, thinking he was singling her out and being hard on her. She felt he should cut her a break. She had a lot on her plate. He was, she decided, wrong in forcing her to comply with their agreement.

Notwithstanding, Dee obliged her boss and this new schedule for a time. The staff seemed to accept this arrangement and did not make waves for John. However, after some weeks went by, Dee began to steal a few minutes here and there on Thursdays. Nina noticed this trend first and informed John.

John confronted Dee on a Friday morning and said, "Strike one, Dee. You left early yesterday."

Dee was angry. She knew John was too busy to notice her early departures and that Nina must have ratted her out. Dee reluctantly forced herself back to the regimen for a time, but subsequently fell back into her bad habits.

"Strike two, Dee," John advised her on another Friday following another breach of their agreement. The third strike did not take long, and on another Friday Dee found herself unemployed.

Two weeks passed since she had been forced to vacate her apartment. Her family had abandoned her. No one even tried to reach out to Dee to see how she was doing following the separation. Dee ran out of money, with not even enough for a meal. One night, succumbing to the hunger pains that were now all too familiar, she decided to visit St. Michael's food kitchen for a hot meal. But as she approached the food kitchen, she could not coax herself onto the line of poor people waiting outside. She walked around the block desperately trying to find the courage and humility to join the line.

Jan Goode had been watching Dee. He manned the outside line of the kitchen as a volunteer. His job was to help move the line along and direct the hungry into the facility for a hot meal. Jan began to notice Dee after her fourth trip past the kitchen and he could see that she was distressed. Jan asked one of the volunteers to take his place momentarily and he walked over to Dee, who was now sitting on the curb with her hands covering her face, sobbing.

"Are you hungry?" Jan asked.

"Excuse me?" she mumbled back.

"I volunteer at the kitchen. I noticed you've been passing by for the past two hours. Why don't you come in for some food?"

"I can't." Dee drew her hands to her face and began to cry. "I can't. I'm, I'm just too humiliated." Dee lost all control and her body shook with her sobs.

Composing herself, she looked up at Jan. "I never thought I'd ever be in this situation. I've done this to myself, you know. I made this all happen. I'm my own worst enemy. I blew a great job with a great boss in a great company." Dee lost her composure again and began to sob, then once again composed herself.

"My boss tried to make me see things as they really were. I just didn't listen to him. I am such a failure in life." Something she said or something about her situation rattled Jan. It all sounded too familiar and brought back some old memories Jan had thought he had long ago erased. This upset Jan. He excused himself and walked back into the kitchen. He emerged a short time later with a container of food for Dee.

"My name is Jan Goode. I understand what you are going through and I think I can help." Jan handed Dee the container.

"Help, me? Do you find people jobs or something?"

"Not exactly." Jan paused and repeated the words a stranger had spoken to him so many years ago, "I'm just a man looking in a very old mirror. Come by the kitchen tomorrow night after close."

Dee spent the night in the bed of a local shelter, pondering the words uttered by Jan. *I'm just a man looking in a very old mirror.* She wondered to herself, *What did it mean?* The words reverberated in her head until sleep arrived.

Dee met with Jan the next night and Jan shared his own story. "A long time ago, I lost my job under circumstances similar to your own. I lost all hope. I was rescued by a stranger who helped me turn my life around."

"How did he help you turn your life around?" Dee implored. Jan shifted in his seat and took a deep breath.

"This individual shared ten principles with me that changed my life forever. I went from unemployed to the CEO of the company that now employs me. Following these laws was not easy. He called them the Rich Habits. But follow them I did, and ten years ago the laws brought me to my current position in life."

"What are these Rich Habits?" Dee asked, in a more demanding, but sincere manner.

"That's not how it works, Dee. You have to go through a training program. When you're sponsored there's no cost. The program will teach you everything you need to know to turn your life around." Jan reached into his pocket and pulled out a pen and paper and jotted a phone number down for Dee. "His name is J.C. Jobs. Call his office in the morning. Tell them Jan Goode sponsored you."

Dee did as Jan advised and secured her place in line at the next session of the Rich Habit Training Program.

The Car Dealer

Herb Riser was in a state of shock. He had just gotten off the phone with his banker and it seemed as if all hope of extending his dealership's floor plan financing had run out. The bank advised him that they were about to enforce their rights under the terms of Herb's credit agreement and repossess his inventory for a subsequent fire sale to limit the bank's losses. For Herb, this meant bankruptcy and financial ruin for his business and, worse, his family.

Driving home that night, he felt so alone. At the light just outside his lot, Herb closed his eyes and let his head drop back. "How did I let this happen?" The words were muffled within the confines of his car. "How am I going to tell my wife?"

He couldn't bear the thought of the anguish he was about to unleash upon his family. They had young children, a large mortgage, and plenty of bills to pay. His employees were no better off with a host of financial obligations of their own. Many of them had taken a chance on Herb, left good jobs to come and work for him, and now this was how they would be repaid. From somewhere behind him, a car honked and Herb opened his eyes to see the green light ahead of him.

Looking to his left, as he eased on the gas, he saw the large lit-up dealership diagonally across the street from his own. That dealership was prospering. Their inventory of vehicles turned every month, while Herb's own inventory grew dusty and worn by the elements. "What does he do differently?" Herb begged for an answer from the great beyond, but his cries went unheard.

Herb had been in the car business for about twenty years. At every dealership that employed Herb, he was the top salesperson. No one even came close to matching Herb's productivity. The man knew how to sell a car. Herb could sell just about anything on the lot, and he knew this, often bragging to coworkers, "I could sell ice to Eskimos." And his success was rewarded. Herb received generous bonuses, and many awards to the dealership trickled down to him in the form of free vacations, Rolex watches, and numerous other items.

Herb turned onto his street, a quiet tree-lined cul-de-sac that backed onto an inlet. The houses were neatly framed by lush manicured lawns and driveways lined with flowerbeds. He pulled to a stop on the road in front of his house. Lights were on in the kitchen and the living room. His family would all be up, his wife cleaning dishes over the sink, the kids watching television, doing homework, or playing. He couldn't tell them; how could he ruin their sense of home and safety? They were expecting him to walk in, heat up some dinner, and talk with them. For them, tonight was a night like any other; but Herb knew that everything was about to change drastically.

At the National Automobile Dealers Association convention several years before, Herb was approached by a dealer he knew from Staten Island. They got to talking and the dealer told Herb that he'd grown tired of traveling to his Mitsubishi franchise in Rhode Island every month to review the month-end financials and create the budget for the following month. He was looking for a buyer and Herb eagerly jumped at the opportunity. He had long dreamed of owning his own store, of running "his" dealership the way he believed a dealership ought to run, making his own rules, and reaping his own rewards. He wanted to be one of the big boys and he saw this opportunity as his long-awaited break.

The first few months in his newly owned car dealership were slow, but that didn't shake Herb's resolve. He attributed the low sales numbers to the ownership transition and was confident that things would soon pick up. He even decided to roll up his sleeves and show his sales team how selling was done by a pro. The numbers picked up a bit, but not the way Herb anticipated. He continued selling day after day, month after month, but sales came hard.

Herb had trouble adjusting to his expanded responsibilities of ownership. Cash flow problems began to occupy more of his time. He found himself visiting banks with increased frequency to add new lines of credit, or strike new floor plan financing arrangements. He spent more time in bank offices than he was spending on the floor of his own showroom, further exacerbating his cash-flow problems. Herb was his own best salesman, even though his numbers paled in comparison to the production he had enjoyed as a salesman at other dealerships. Juggling management responsibilities along with sales was proving too much.

Herb got out of his car and stepped into the cold night air. He flexed his fingers inside his tight black leather gloves and the moon glinted off the face of the Rolex watch he won years ago after setting an annual sales record at a previous dealership he worked for. Now he stood on the porch of his home feeling like an intruder, the person who was about to come in and shatter his family's world. He couldn't do it, not just yet. Herb sat down in the old wicker rocking chair on the porch and collected his thoughts. He wasn't ready.

Herb was not a student of the auto industry. For him the business of running a car dealership was all about one thing: sales. Customers were merely prospects to be conquered. "Overcome objections at all costs," he often told other salesman. "The customer doesn't make a decision to buy; we do that for them. That's our job."

Oftentimes, and reluctantly, the owner at Herb's last dealership had to act as a mediator on behalf of a customer who felt they were being treated rudely by Herb. His boss knew Herb could sell, that was clear from the numbers, but Herb didn't really understand the bigger picture.

"Herb, we're not interested in just the sale. We want these customers for life and we want their kids, and their kids' kids. This dealership goes to great lengths to provide them with the products they want and the quality service they can expect from us. Without them and their continued business we'd be finished. You are by far the best salesman I have ever had, but sometimes you focus solely on the sale and you forget that there is a whole lot more to making money here than just selling a car," Herb's boss explained in a private meeting after a customer felt particularly bullied by Herb's aggressive selling techniques.

Herb's hand rested on the front-door handle. His fingers gripped the knob. Just beyond the door he could hear the kids running around upstairs, laughing. He closed his eyes and let the sound of laughter fill his ears, letting his forehead fall to the door. He sniffed once, the tip of his nose burning in the cold night air, and pushed open the front door.

"Herb?" his wife called from the kitchen. "You're late tonight; I saved you a plate."

Herb slid out of his coat and hung it in the foyer, carefully tucking his gloves into the pocket. He reluctantly strolled into the kitchen and sank into one of the chairs around the table. His wife was putting together his dinner, but he wasn't hungry.

"You all right?" she inquired, noticing Herb's demeanor. Normally, when he arrived home he was more animated, happy to be home with his family after the long workday.

"I have to tell you something," Herb said. He would do this quickly. He took a deep breath and began.

"What are we going to do?" his wife asked, slumping against the counter when Herb finished telling her everything. Her face was blank and her eyes fixed somewhere faraway. Herb couldn't bear to look at her.

"How will we pay the mortgage?" she whispered, more to herself than to her husband. She began to cry and Herb's heart was breaking. Upstairs he could hear his children stomping around their bedrooms, boisterous and lively. Downstairs the kitchen was filled with sobbing.

Somehow, Herb dragged himself out of bed the next morning. In the mirror he could see his reflection shave, brush his reflection's teeth, and run a comb through his reflection's hair. He felt like he was watching someone else from a million miles away. When he got to his dealership it didn't take long for his staff to sense that something was wrong. Herb shut himself in his office and avoided conversing with anyone for most of the day. He was desperately trying to think his way out of this whole mess, but for all his thinking, he kept coming up short. Numerous calls to his banker went unanswered and unreturned.

The floor was quiet most of the day. Very few prospects walked through the showroom and the service department closed early that evening due to a lack of business. When most of the staff had departed, Herb came down from his upstairs office and began his nightly ritual of closing the shop.

A woman in her mid-fifties walked through the front doors just as Herb was making his way from the service desk toward the showroom to lock up. Herb was slightly startled, seeing her standing by the reception desk.

"May I help you?" Herb asked in a melancholy tone.

"I'm looking for a car for my daughter. She is graduating from Brown next month and I was hoping to surprise her," the woman gushed. "Do you have any convertibles?"

For a moment, the salesman in Herb stirred, but he suppressed the urge. "I'm sorry; I won't be able to help you."

"Well, how about an SUV then? It doesn't necessarily have to be a convertible."

Herb stared at the woman and felt himself shrinking. "I mean I won't be able to sell you *any* car because I won't be able to provide service support."

"I don't understand."

Herb swallowed hard before continuing, "After this month, we will most likely no longer be in business, I'm afraid." Herb's eyes dropped from her face to the floor, ashamed. "We won't be here to service your daughter's car or provide any follow-up support. I'm very sorry. I can't help you. I can't help anyone."

Herb tried to usher the woman towards the door, but she didn't move. "Wait," she said, taking a step towards him, a look of compassion blanketed her face. "Tell me what happened?"

Herb looked at her, startled by the request, and considered it for a moment. He figured he had nothing to lose at that point. *Why not?* he thought to himself. Herb offered her a chair at a nearby desk and spilled the whole story. He held nothing back. He was brutally honest about his failings. Unknown to Herb, his bankruptcy story was a familiar one to the woman, who had gone through her own bankruptcy a long, long time ago.

"What is your name?" she asked once he had finished his story.

"Herb Riser," he shook his head, embarrassed, before offering his hand. He had told this woman his whole sad story before even exchanging introductions.

"I'm Susan Changer," she replied, shaking firmly. "I'd like to help you."

"You want to help me?" Herb replied in disbelief. "Why?"

Susan repeated the words someone said to her many years ago, "I'm just a person looking in a very old mirror." Susan began to share her own story of failure and the redemption she received from an individual by the name of J.C. Jobs. "Here is J.C.'s office number. I want you to call them in the morning. Just let them know I sponsored you. That gets you into the next training session for free."

They shook hands and parted ways. Herb eyed the phone number as Susan walked out the doors of his dealership. *Who is this J.C. Jobs?* he closed his eyes and wondered to himself. *I sure do hope he can perform miracles, because that's what I need. A miracle.* With his eyes still closed and his hands unconsciously wrapped around the piece of paper with J.C. Job's number on it, Herb looked as if he was praying.

The Accountant

Tears flowed down his cheeks as he dropped a red rose on to the casket below. His was the last rose. With that final act, the crowd of mourners began to disburse and the accountant was now alone with his three young children, standing over Denise's casket, staring mindlessly into the open grave and loathing himself.

"It's called cervical intraepithelial neoplasia," Denise had said. She had sat down at the kitchen table and poured him a fresh cup of coffee. The coffee sat steaming between them, untouched. "The doctor recommended surgery to correct the disorder."

"Surgery?" He stared nervously at her. The sun fell across the table in wide slats, angled through the blinds. Beyond the glass he could see a cloudless blue sky stretching across the backyard. Suddenly he felt like he was falling from that sky, endlessly falling. Denise looked calm, as though she was going over a grocery list with him. Denise never fumbled. Even though this was a very serious matter, she had a way of dealing with the illness in a relaxed, calm manner. Denise had always been the pragmatic, rational one, in control in the relationship. She hardly ever got worked up the way he did.

"I asked if the surgery was absolutely necessary and he seemed to waver." Denise threw her left hand in the air in a dismissive fashion. "He said I didn't need to have the surgery done right away, but there were certain risks if the problem were to remain uncorrected indefinitely." Denise rested her chin casually in her hand, as though she were recalling memories of a recent holiday, or chatting about a neighbor's new kitchen. Her poise amazed him.

"Get the surgery, Denise, please."

"Oh, 'please' yourself; you know we can't afford the surgery. Our insurance is ridiculous; the deductible is way too high."

"If you need the surgery, you need the surgery," he pleaded with her. He brought his hand to his mouth and shook his head, trying to clear his mind of the image of a sick Denise. He forced himself to focus on her as she was here and now. She looked like his Denise, the same woman he had wed nearly twenty years ago, although now, slightly plump, with the hint of a smile always dancing behind her eyes, vibrant and alive. She couldn't be sick, not Denise.

"We can't afford the surgery just now and we certainly can't afford for me to be incapacitated," Denise demanded. "We just don't have the five-thousand dollars right now. The surgery will just have to wait."

He dropped his hand to the table and let out an audible, exhausted groan. Her fingers crept over the tabletop and came to rest atop his hand, warm, soft and comforting. She squeezed tightly in an effort to reassure him. "It can wait until after tax season. We'll have money then." She smiled at him.

About three months later, while the accountant was in the heart of tax season, an unfortunate ritual that was the nature of his profession, Denise's condition worsened. Her spotting became more frequent but she chose not to concern her husband, who was working sixteen-hour days and weekends. She knew he had hundreds of clients with hundreds of tax returns that needed to be filed within the next six weeks. Denise decided not to bother him until after tax season, when they would have some additional cash and could afford the operation to fix her problem. That operation never did happen. Denise's illness turned to cancer and it spread like wildfire. She lasted through the summer, and passed away in a hospital bed, leaving behind a shattered husband and their three children. Denise, a kind, devoted wife and mother, was no more.

The accountant staggered through his work and his new job as a single parent. It was nearly a year before the fog began to lift and he regained some level of clear-headedness. Denise's sudden death left him angry and confused. He blamed himself for that and for their financial plight. These self-recriminations continued until one morning after a vivid dream in which Denise spoke to him, saying, "All you need to do is ask the right questions." The words burned in the accountant's ears through most of that day and stayed with him that night until he fell asleep.

A newness of thought woke with him that next morning. "Why am I doing badly while so many of my clients, the clients who ask me for financial advice, are doing so well?" he asked himself as he rubbed the sleep from his eyes. "It can't be a matter of knowledge. I know far more in terms of tax and finances than any of my clients. There must be something I am doing wrong that *they are doing right!*"

The accountant determined then and there to uncover their secrets. One of the first things he did was to create a list of questions to ask his successful clients in an effort to find out what they did that he didn't. His list evolved and changed over time into twenty questions. He awoke one night with the thought that he should also take this list of questions to his unsuccessful clients to see if there were differences between their answers and those of his wealthy clients. The U.S. Patent Office refers to such extraordinary human thoughts and ideas as "flashes of genius." Until that night, it had never occurred to the accountant that the answers he obtained from his successful clients only had relevance if they could be compared to the answers of his unsuccessful clients.

What was initially a relatively simple, short-term project became a five-year obsession with analysis and discovery in studying the data he gathered from the two diverse groups. The conclusion was astounding. There was a difference the size of the Grand Canyon between the answers he received from his successful clients and the answers he received from his unsuccessful clients.

As an example, when he asked the question, "What do you do when you leave your office?" the answers given by his successful clients reflected that, as a group, they were engaged in numerous social or business activities. Some served on different boards, others were involved in speaking engagements; some taught; some were involved with their church; some were seeking advanced degrees related to their professions; some continued working in their home offices; some ran little league clubs, and some were involved in volunteer work for non-profit organizations. When this question was asked of the unsuccessful group of clients, their answers were strikingly uniform. They ate dinner, watched television or engaged in some recreational activity, went to bed, and repeated the same routine the next day. The accountant's epiphany was that he had uncovered the secret to financial success, which he could see was embodied in the daily habits of successful people.

Excited by his discovery, he categorized his findings, which he eventually narrowed down into easy to understand principles that came to be known as "Rich Habits."

The accountant incorporated these habits into his daily life. For thirty days he diligently followed his Rich Habits list. Each and every day, in the morning, at noon, and just before bed, he went over his list. Opportunities began to manifest seemingly out of thin air. His revenue began to increase. New clients came through his office doors. He had to hire new employees to meet the demands of his new clients. The accountant was roused to such heights of excitement that he could hardly contain himself. He felt as if he had just imbibed some magical elixir that was transforming his life.

Shortly after incorporating the Rich Habits into his daily life, an old client called who had been struggling with serious cash flow problems.

"I need you to help me secure another line with a bank," the client asked over the phone. "I desperately need another fifty-thousand dollars. If I don't get this money, I'm finished. I won't be able to make payroll next month or pay my vendors."

It seemed to the accountant that, since he first met his client, the man was always struggling with cash flow. A thought flashed through his mind. "I'll tell you what," the accountant offered, "I'll help you secure the additional financing for free but I want something from you. Come in next week and I'll explain further." The accountant hung up the phone and during the next week set out to develop a workable program based upon his Rich Habits, so that he could share them with his unfortunate client.

The following week the two met in his office. "What's this?" The client was puzzling over the papers that lay before him.

"This is an agreement," the accountant replied.

"For what?" the client asked, as he began to study the lead document, which read as follows:

"I herein agree to diligently follow the attached Program for thirty days. In exchange, all fees associated with securing additional financing will be waived."

The client considered the document for a few moments and browsed through the program the accountant created just for him.

"That's all I have to do? Follow this program for thirty days?"

A slight smile spread across the accountant's face. "Thirty days."

"Seems simple enough." The client signed the document.

"Are you ready to begin?" the accountant asked enthusiastically.

"Now? I... I... I guess so," the client stammered.

With that, J.C. Jobs pulled a copy of the Rich Habits Training Program toward his client and opened to the first page.

The Rich Habits
Training Program

Before beginning the Rich Habits Training Program it is necessary to dispel a common myth about financial success with regard to luck. Many unsuccessful people rationalize that they don't have "good luck" or just aren't "lucky." They argue that in order to be financially successful you need good luck. Is good luck important to becoming successful? The answer is a resounding "Yes!" All successful people have experienced good luck. In fact, no one will ever become successful if they do not have some good luck. But let's elaborate on this truth.

There are four types of luck. The first type of luck is "random good luck." This is a type of good luck we have no control over, like winning the lottery or receiving an unexpected inheritance.

The second type of luck is "random bad luck." Like random good luck, we have no control over this, either. Events creating this type of luck are outside of our influence for the most part. Examples include coming down with a disease, getting hit by lightning, random accidents, a tree falling on your house, etc.

The third type of luck is "opportunity luck." This is good luck that is a byproduct of good daily habits. Think of opportunity luck as an apple orchard. You prepare the land, plant the apple seeds, and diligently nurture the trees as they grow. After some time the apple trees blossom and bear fruit. This fruit is the byproduct of doing the things you needed to do over a long period of time. These apples represent opportunity luck.

Successful people do the things that are necessary over the long term in order for opportunity luck to occur in their lives. They live the Rich Habits every single day. Rich Habits are like a magnet for opportunity luck. Many of the opportunities are completely unexpected. Some people refer to this as "the law of attraction." Opportunity luck follows the law of attraction for those who live the Rich Habits.

The fourth type of luck is "detrimental luck." Detrimental luck is the evil twin of opportunity luck. Unsuccessful people have bad habits. Like the Rich Habits, bad habits are also seeds. They will take root and grow until they too bear fruit. Unfortunately, the bad fruit birthed by bad habits brings detrimental luck into the lives of the unsuccessful. This detrimental luck might be a job loss, investment losses, foreclosure, divorce, illness, or something similar.

To bring success into your life you need to attract the right kind of luck. Living the Rich Habits guarantees you will attract the right kind of luck, and opportunities will appear, seemingly out of thin air. As with low-hanging fruit, all you have to do is reach out and pick it.

Rich Habit Promise Number One:

I will form good daily habits and follow these good daily habits every day.

Good daily habits are the foundation of success. Successful people differ from unsuccessful people in their daily habits. Successful people have many good and few bad daily habits. Unsuccessful people have many bad and few good daily habits. Most successful people are not even aware that they possess such habits. This is why defining success has always been difficult.

No person will ever be successful until they can identify their strengths and weaknesses. Self-assessment requires brutal honesty. But how does one define a given strength or weakness? This is not an easy task, as it is often too nebulous a request. We get in our own way. Our egos interfere and we are left with an uncertainty about the accuracy of our own analysis. It is much easier for a third party to assess us than for us to assess ourselves.

A simple and foolproof approach to assessing ourselves is to look at our daily patterns of living, our daily habits. By recognizing our daily habits we gain keener insights into our individual strengths and weaknesses. Understanding that our own bad daily habits are preventing us from becoming successful represents the first and most significant step on the path toward financial success.

On a piece of paper, form two columns. List your Bad Daily Habits under column one. Invert each one of your Bad Daily Habits and list their opposites under column two, which we'll refer to as your new Good Daily Habits.

See example on the next page:

Bad Daily Habits	Good Daily Habits
I watch too much television.	I limit myself to one hour of TV per day.
I don't exercise regularly.	I exercise thirty minutes each day.
I don't watch what I eat.	I eat no more than XXXX calories per day.
I don't do my work-related reading.	I read thirty minutes each day.
I procrastinate.	I complete items on my to-do list every day.
I waste too much time on the Internet.	I limit my daily recreational Internet use.
I smoke.	I will not smoke today.
I don't return phone calls right away.	I will return every phone call today.
I don't remember names.	I write down names and remember them.
I forget important dates.	I acknowledge dates that are important to others.

For thirty days follow your new Good Daily Habits. Review them once in the morning, once at noon, and once at bedtime. In this way, each and every day, hold yourself accountable for following them. The objective is to complete at least eighty percent of your Good Daily Habits each day.

Good Daily Habits Work Week Checklist (Sample Items)

1. I read industry-related material a half-hour today.
2. I ran 30 minutes today.
3. I completed 80% of my to-do list today.
4. I called at least one prospect today.
5. I did not waste time on the Internet today.
6. I said "DO IT NOW" when I did not want to do something today.
7. I stopped myself from saying something sarcastic today.
8. I stopped myself from saying something inappropriate today.
9. I stopped myself from talking today when I realized I was talking too much.
10. I ate no more than 2,000 calories today.
11. I limited myself to two beers today.
12. I left the office after 6 p.m. today.
13. I called one person today, just to say hello.
14. I called someone today to wish him or her a happy birthday.

Summary:

Successful people are slaves to their good daily habits. This is the first Rich Habit and the most important Rich Habit.

Rich Habit Promise Number Two:

I will set goals for each day, for each month, for each year and for the long-term. I will focus on my goals each and every day.

Successful people are goal-oriented. They create goals all the time. Daily goals are represented in their daily to-do lists. Long-term goals are broad initiatives to be accomplished at specified points. Successful people focus on work at work, and leave their family and personal matters outside the office in an effort to achieve their business goals.

Successful people are long-term thinkers. They are constantly looking to the future in an effort to determine where they are in terms of accomplishing their goals. They do not dwell on the past – no daydreaming about past successes or failures. They continuously make course corrections to get back on track in achieving their goals.

Unsuccessful people are not goal-oriented. Like leaves on a fall day, they float in the air aimlessly, without direction. They allow the distractions of daily living to affect their ability to perform their duties at work. They allow themselves to become easily distracted by things that have nothing to do with their work. Since they are not focused on goals, they have nothing grounding them to the tasks they need to perform to become successful.

Daily Goals

Before beginning each day, compile a Daily Goal/To-do List. List only those things that have a realistic probability (eighty percent chance) of being completed that day. Prioritize this list and set a specific time in which to tackle each item. The lower-priority items are those that have a low probability (bottom twenty percent) of being accomplished that day and can be accomplished the subsequent day. Do this in order to build flexibility into the to-do list and avoid the frustration of failing to accomplish the important tasks set for that day. During the day, mark off each completed task and congratulate yourself in its accomplishment. At the end of the day evaluate the to-do list. This forces accountability.

Rich Habits Daily Goals/To-Do List (Sample Week Day)

Description	When
Profession-related reading.	6-6:30 A.M.
Check voicemail and email.	8:30 A.M.
Call one person just to say hello.	9:00 A.M.
Make Happy Birthday calls/emails.	9:00 A.M.
Call prospect list.	9:30 A.M.
Complete pending Life Insurance applications.	10:00 A.M.
Follow-up on pending cases.	11:00 A.M.
Client meetings.	1-5 P.M.
Return all phone calls.	5:00 P.M.
End-of-day prospect calling.	5:30 P.M.

In the above example, completing eight out of ten Daily Goals for the day is considered successful.

Monthly Goals

At the beginning of each month, list monthly goals. These are goals with a realistic probability of being reached by the end of the month. Break down each goal into tasks or steps. The monthly goals could be the number of insurance policies to write that month, or the number of new clients you hope to gain, or a revenue target for the month. These goals might include a project to be completed or an article to be written.

EXAMPLE - MONTHLY GOAL NUMBER ONE: I will write five life insurance policies this month. In order to achieve this goal I will need to meet with ten prospects each week for the next four weeks. In order for these meetings to occur, I will make fifty phone calls each week, which breaks down into ten calls each day.

Goals for the Current Year and the Following Year

Goals for the current year and for the following year represent initiatives that you have some degree of control over achieving. Break down each goal into tasks that need to be accomplished.

EXAMPLE – CURRENT YEAR GOAL NUMBER ONE: I will pass the CPA exam this year. In order to reach this goal I will study. I will establish a study plan in which I will study one hour each day during the week and six hours over each weekend. I will review the study material and complete the practice exams.

Long-term Goals

Long-term goals represent broad, far-reaching initiatives. Think of your long-term goals as your "wish list." Create a plan for accomplishing each goal and include the tasks needed to be accomplished.

EXAMPLE – LONG-TERM GOAL NUMBER ONE: I will buy a house in five years. In order to reach this goal I will save one thousand dollars per month for the next five years. In order to save one thousand dollars per month I will reduce my expenses and deposit two-hundred-and-fifty dollars each pay period into a separate savings account.

Rich Habits Goal Sheet

Current Year Goals	Next Year's Goals	Long-Term Goals
Take CPA Exam	Write and Publish Book	Make $....Within Five Years
Obtain Long-Term Care Designation	Increase Savings Another $....	Buy Convertible For My Wife
Increase Savings Account by $....	Take CFP Exam	Become a Partner by....
Pay Off Car Loan	Get My Weight Down to 180 Pounds	Pay Off Mortgage by....
Lose Ten Pounds by....	Run Marathon	Buy Beach House by....
Obtain Promotion to	Increase Salary to....	Accumulate $.... In College Savings For My Children

A useful technique to assist in keeping long-term goals in sight is the use of a vision board. A vision board is an actual picture of long-term goals. This may be a picture of the house you desire to buy, a picture of the business you hope to own one day, or a picture of the type of place you hope to retire to one day. Before he rose to great fame, comedian Jim Carey wrote out a check to himself for twenty million dollars and kept that check in a place where he would see it every day. That check represented a vision board of a long-term goal he desired to achieve one day – to be paid twenty million dollars for a movie. When the opportunity arose for a leading role in a movie, guess what Jim Carey's demand for compensation was? Twenty million dollars. And he got it!

Summary:

Successful people set goals and create a plan to reach those goals.

Rich Habit Promise Number Three:

I will engage in self-improvement every day.

Successful people engage in the process of self-improvement every day. They read industry periodicals and technical material specific to their profession or trade. They become students of their industry, profession, or trade, and keep current with changes that occur. They do not spend excessive amounts of non-work time watching television, or surfing the Internet.

Successful people read for self-improvement. They are perpetual students. Each day they devote blocks of time to better themselves by studying subject matter that will improve them in some way and better enable them to perform their jobs. Time is too valuable to be wasted on matters with no tangible value. They coordinate their goals with self-improvement and set specific goals. This may involve obtaining an additional license, a degree, or developing a new niche for their business. They are continuously engaged in some constructive project to increase their skill sets, promote their business or careers, keep their minds sharp, or expand their business prospects.

Unsuccessful people are not students of their industry, profession, or trade. They do not routinely follow their industry. They do not regularly read industry periodicals. They would rather spend hours each day watching television or engaged in "junk" reading. They use rationalization to justify their negligence in improving themselves.

Self-improvement involves engaging is some activity every day that will improve your mind and expand your knowledge to better your career. Expanding knowledge within your industry is a self-improvement activity that you must engage in. This can be done by regularly reading your industry periodicals and advancing your career by obtaining additional licenses, skill sets, or new niches for your business. Career-specific self-improvement activities are necessary to increase skills and take advantage of opportunities. You will notice that, as your knowledge base grows, opportunities begin to present themselves.

Choose a time when there are fewer distractions and you can set aside a block of time. Sometimes this is possible in the early morning hours, prior to beginning your normal workday. At a minimum, set aside thirty minutes each day for these activities. Thirty minutes per day may not seem like much, but over time, it adds up to a significant amount of self-improvement activity. No matter what time of the day works best for you, engage in daily self-improvement activities without interruptions.

Summary:

Successful people devote time each and every day to self-improvement.

Rich Habit Promise Number Four:

I will devote part of each and every day in caring for my health.

Successful people make a concerted effort to eat right and exercise every day. They consider not only what they eat, but also how much they eat. They manage their consumption of food. Successful people do not binge or overindulge in food or drink. If they do slip, it is managed overindulgence, relegated to that of an infrequent occurrence rather than a regular occurrence, such as a holiday meal or a party.

For successful people, exercise is a routine, like brushing their teeth. They understand that daily exercise improves their bodies and minds. Routine exercise improves the immune system and results in fewer sick days. This further allows for an increase in productivity, since the frequency of sick days is less than that of others. People who regularly exercise generally have more energy during the day.

Successful people have a system or routine for weight management that works best for them. Some have sophisticated systems, some less sophisticated, but they "manage" their weight. Managing weight means monitoring the amount of food consumed every day and engaging in a daily exercise regimen.

Unsuccessful people have no consistent, day-to-day control over their health. They are always in search of the latest and greatest quick-fix diet idea. Unsuccessful people deal with health matters sporadically and usually require outside influences to motivate them to eat less or eat differently. This is the reason why there are so many diet books out there. With little control over their eating habits, they go through phases of gaining and losing weight again and again. This behavior takes a toll on the body, which eventually manifest as medical disorders, such as high blood pressure, diabetes, heart disease, and the like.

Unsuccessful people approach exercise the same way they approach their consumption of food, requiring some outside force to momentarily motivate them. When that motivation wears off, they fall back into bad habits, stop exercising, and gain weight as part of a cycle that recurs throughout their lives.

An easy way to monitor food consumption is to count the calories after every meal or snack, and document daily consumption. In beginning a weight management program, first gain an understanding of the specific foods you eat on a daily basis. During the first thirty days of your weight management program you will need to track what you normally eat and figure out the number of calories for each food item. During this thirty day period you will be able to identify certain foods that are high in calories and you can thereafter choose to avoid those high-calorie foods, at least on a regular basis.

Do not confuse monitoring and managing food consumption with dieting. They are not the same. Diets don't work in managing weight in the long term. The reason is that they are too restrictive, unsustainable and, quite frankly, take the fun out of life. Managing the consumption of food does not mean starving or never again eating special treats. You are going to eat treats from time to time and you should not feel guilty about this. You simply need to understand that you can't eat those high-calorie foods every day, as this will likely push you over your daily caloric threshold, which is the threshold you need to stay within in order to lose or maintain your weight. You should be free to eat and drink the things you like when the spirit moves you. But you need to understand that eating some of the foods you love might mean occasionally exceeding your caloric threshold for that day, which is fine as long as this is the exception rather than the rule.

Monitoring food consumption only gets you halfway toward managing weight. You must engage in a daily aerobic exercise regimen for at least twenty to thirty minutes a day, four days per week. Jogging outdoors provides the most effective results. The number of calories burned with running is greater by about one-third than an indoor treadmill, Stairmaster, or stationary bike. Lifting weights, sit-ups, push-ups, and the like, are good supplements to any basic aerobic activity, but they are not substitutes for aerobic activity. By themselves, these exercises will not help you lose weight as much as they will help you shape and tone your body. Aerobic activity is the most reliable activity to help you lose weight and should be the foundation for your exercise regimen.

Morning may be the best time to engage in exercise activity. By preceding the work day, you are less likely to be pulled away by scheduling issues or conflicts that often occur during the day.

A great tool to monitor your weight is the Rich Habits Weight Management Tracking Schedule. Tracking takes only five minutes each day. You will begin to see patterns in your weight management that enable you to better understand your body and allow you to gain control over your weight. Within two months of completing the Rich Habits Weight Management Tracking Schedule (see next page) you will be able to determine your individual daily caloric threshold and you can then manage your calorie intake to lose or maintain your weight. For example, assume your daily threshold is 2,100 calories per day, given the level of exercise you do. If you consume less than 2,100 calories each day, you will lose weight every day.

Summary:

Successful people manage their consumption of food and engage in regular exercise.

Rich Habits Weight Management Tracking Schedule

| START WEIGHT |
| GOAL WEIGHT |
| END WEIGHT |

CALORIC THRESHOLD ------->

DATE		WEIGHT	AEROBIC ACTIVITY TIME	BREAKFAST CALORIES	LUNCH CAL.	DINNER CAL.	TOTAL CAL.	CUMU-LATIVE CAL.	AVE. CAL.
SUN.	1/1								
MON.	1/2								
TUES.	1/3								
WED.	1/4								
THURS.	1/5								
FRI.	1/6								
SAT.	1/7								
SUN..	1/8								
MON.	1/9								
TUES.	1/10								
WED.	1/11								
THURS.	1/12								
FRI.	1/13								
SAT.	1/14								
SUN.	1/15								
MON.	1/16								
TUES.	1/17								
WED.	1/18								
THURS.	1/19								
FRI.	1/20								
SAT.	1/21								
SUN.	1/22								
MON.	1/23								
TUES.	1/24								
WED.	1/25								
THURS.	1/26								
FRI.	1/27								
SAT.	1/28								
SUN.	1/29								
MON.	1/30								
TUES.	1/31								

MONTH	AEROBIC DAYS	MINUTES	MILES	AVG CALORIES	LBS (LOST)/GAINED	START WEIGHT	END WEIGHT
JAN.					-		
FEB.					-		
MAR.					-		
APRIL					-		
MAY					-		
JUNE					-		
JULY					-		
AUG.					-		
SEPT.					-		
OCT.					-		
NOV.					-		
DEC.					-		

Rich Habit Promise Number Five:

I will devote each and every day to forming lifelong relationships.

To successful people, relationships are like gold. They tend to relationships like a farmer tends crops, nurturing them every day, remembering names, birthdays, gifts for newborns, and interacting frequently. Successful people seek to help their relationships and their business associates, even when there is nothing in it for them. They are focused on others, rather than on themselves.

For successful people, networking is a prerequisite to their success. They develop systems and processes as tools to assist them in networking efforts. They search for reasons to reach out to their contacts, such as birthday contacts or congratulatory calls, cards, or gifts. They attend important celebrations and milestones such as graduations, funerals, and weddings. They network with individuals who are like-minded. They do not waste their time developing and nurturing relationships with individuals who are only out for themselves. They cut all ties that are harmful or destructive, and stay clear of individuals who are perpetually in a state of turmoil. Many times this turmoil is financial in nature. These individuals have bad habits and often drag down their friends or associates.

Successful people are students of relationship building. They faithfully return phone calls right away. They continuously seek out ways to improve their relationships.

Unsuccessful people have a "What have you done for me lately?" attitude about relationships. Some, oddly enough, even consider it a virtue when they intentionally shortchange others. If an individual cannot provide them with some immediate value, they are ignored until needed. No calls, emails, or cards on birthdays. No gifts congratulating their "friends" or associates on the important events in their lives. Unsuccessful people are not good networkers. They don't seek to improve their relationships with others on a continuous and regular basis. They do not return phone calls right away, and sometimes not at all.

Unsuccessful people adopt a "put out the fire" mindset in managing relationships. When a crisis arises, and unsuccessful people often have sudden crises in their lives, they reach out for help. Oftentimes, they seek assistance from an individual they have neglected. When it comes to relationships, unsuccessful people simply do not care enough to invest time in developing relationships.

Successful people employ a system in managing their relationships. Some have systems that can be quite sophisticated and utilize the latest in technology and software. Whatever system you create for yourself, find a way to track various types of information about each of your contacts. Besides names, addresses, phone numbers, and email information, capture other important data such as: professions; birthdays; spouse names; spouse birthdays; names of children; college, graduate school, law school etc.; hobbies, interests, and other important data. "Important" means important to your contact. The most common contact management system is Outlook. Almost anyone with a computer has Outlook. Some cell phones even link up with Outlook, giving you the ability to carry contact information with you.

Having the greatest contact management system in the world does you no good unless you put your system to good use. The most basic system provides a process that reminds you of a contact's birthday so you can reach out to them to wish them a happy birthday. Even if you do not regularly communicate with a specific person, this minimum amount of contact keeps your relationship alive. Birthday calls allow you to maintain a relationship by being in touch at least once a year. Your contact may reciprocate, thus increasing the frequency of your contacts with this individual to two times per year.

I have never met a successful person who has not shared with me the same nasty little secret…each of us has difficulty remembering names. To overcome this failing, successful people create a system to help them remember names of even the most remote contacts.

A good way to remember names is to group your contacts by category. For example you can group contacts into the following categories:

Tennis contacts
Golf contacts
Bowling contacts
Club contacts
Neighbor contacts
Friend John Smith's friends
College friends
Spouse's college friends
Business partner's friends
Work associates and their families
Church/synagogue/mosque, or community contacts, etc.

Before any event in which you are likely to run into one or more of your contacts you can pull out that category's group of contacts and review their names just before you go to the event. Names are important to each one of us and we all appreciate when someone feels we're important enough to be remembered by name.

Summary:

Successful people foster, grow, and improve their relationships with others each and every day. They devote significant amounts of time networking.

Rich Habit Promise Number Six:

I will live each and every day in a state of moderation.

To live in moderation means to live a balanced life – no extremes. Successful people avoid excesses, wild emotional swings, addictions, obsessions, binging, starvation, extravagances, and fanatical behavior. They keep their thoughts and emotions on a short leash. They understand the need to be on an even keel and in control of their lives.

Successful people do not binge, cram, over indulge, or behave in an excessive manner. They understand that life is a marathon and not a sprint. They moderate their work hours, eating habits, exercise, alcohol intake, watching television, reading, Internet use, phone conversations, emails, text messages, conversations, entertainment, sexual relations, and so on. Their personalities reflect this moderate mindset. They do not become overly excited or excessively melancholy. They are even-tempered, and slow to anger or excitement. Their moderate mindset puts family, friends, colleagues, and business partners at ease, which helps improve relationships. As a consequence, people enjoy being around them. There is a comfort level in dealing with them in all matters.

Successful people eat, drink, entertain, and live moderate lifestyles. Contrary to what many believe, and as a general rule, their homes, cars, personal effects, vacations, etc., are not extravagant. Warren Buffet, one of the wealthiest individuals in the world, has lived in the same home he was married in more than fifty years ago. His home is modest with no fence or surrounding wall. While he owns a private jet business, he flies commercial airlines. He drives back and forth to work in his car every day. Warren Buffet lives this Rich Habit on a daily basis.

Unsuccessful people live in extremes. They eat too much and drink too much. They overreact to events. They permit their emotions to swing in extreme manners, which create great conflict and pain in their relationships. Emotions such as anger, happiness, love, hate, jealousy, and envy are placed on a very long leash, perhaps reeled in momentarily when their most important relationships are placed in jeopardy. They obsess over food, drink, sex, drugs, gossip, personal possessions, their opinions, their thoughts, and their actions.

Unsuccessful people have little control over their lives. They have wild swings in their moods, which result in strained health, strained relationships, and strained finances. They have a "keep up with the Jones" mindset. Their spending patterns are continuously influenced by others. If they fall into money somehow, they spend this money on big homes and expensive cars to impress others. Mortgages and loans stretch them financially. Many refinance their homes in an effort to maintain their lifestyles. An unexpected event, such as a job loss, temporary disability, or sudden decline in earnings, results in immediate financial catastrophe because unsuccessful people live paycheck to paycheck. They have no savings or financial safety net. Their priorities are misplaced. They are incapable of living moderate lifestyles, prioritizing their needs correctly, or living within their means.

Summary:

Successful people do everything in moderation.

Rich Habit Promise Number Seven:

I will accomplish my daily tasks each and every day. I will adopt a "do it now" mindset.

Successful people do not procrastinate. They do not put off until tomorrow what they can do today. They are focused on accomplishing things. They create "to-do" lists to record and plan the accomplishments desired for each day. They understand the need to be the ones controlling their lives. They do not let life or events control them. As a result, they are responsive to clients, patients, business partners, family, and friends.

Successful people are goal-oriented. They set goals and achieve them. They are constantly completing tasks and projects in a timely manner. They are proactive. Consequently, they are not engaged in the practice of putting out fires or dealing with emergencies. They ignore the voice of procrastination.

Unsuccessful people procrastinate. They delay, put off, and defer things that should and could be done that very day. Their procrastination creates problems that require immediate attention. Procrastination increases the risk of forgetting something important, or dealing with a critical matter in an emergency setting, which risks mistakes, errors, and legal liabilities that can result in lawsuits. Procrastination leads to poor quality in whatever service they provide. The lives of unsuccessful people are haphazard, confused, and complicated. They cannot accomplish much as they are constantly putting out one fire after another. They react instead to outside forces, which command their immediate attention. They have no control over their lives or their daily schedules. They feel powerless and directionless.

Do not procrastinate or delay in activities that should be performed in a given day. When the thought of putting off something enters your mind, immediately cast this thought out by saying, "Do It Now." Repeat these three words a hundred times a day if necessary. Do not allow thoughts of procrastination even a second of life. Once you are fully engaged in an activity, you will soon find yourself absorbed in the activity and all thoughts of deferring the task will be gone. You will feel exhilarated in accomplishing the task and feel in control of your life.

Summary:

Successful people do not procrastinate and have a "Do It Now" mindset.

Rich Habit Promise Number Eight:

I will engage in rich thinking every day.

Successful people are positive, enthusiastic, energetic, happy, and well-balanced individuals. They feel powerful, in control, confident, and energized. This is not by accident. They are disciples of Rich Thinking. When they talk to themselves, their words are uplifting, not critical. They congratulate themselves internally all the time. They use positive affirmations every day to reinforce their attitudes and create a positive mindset. They do not get down on themselves when problems occur. They have adopted the Rich Thinking that problems and obstacles are opportunities.

Successful people control their thoughts and emotions. Bad thoughts are displaced immediately by good thoughts. They understand that allowing a bad thought even a second of life will permit the bad thought to take root and eventually change their behavior in a negative way. They feed their minds with positive, good thoughts, and let them take root, eventually blossoming, and one day bearing fruit.

Successful people think rich thoughts every day. They use positive affirmations and visualization techniques to drive and alter their mindset. Contrary to what you may believe, successful people have dire thoughts enter their minds. How could they not, with all of the negative news that we are constantly bombarded with from the various media outlets? Every day we are bombarded with bad thoughts. The information we absorb causes fear, anxiety, angst, and it is easy to fall victim to this barrage of negativity. Successful people realize this and try to minimize their consumption of television, radio programming, or Internet sites that are negative. Rather, they watch or listen to programming that is constructive or uplifting. They read positive newspaper or magazine articles and stay away from the negative ones. Successful people control what they see and hear every day.

Lastly, successful people are grateful for all that life has given them. They express thanks every day, oftentimes before sleep or upon waking in the morning. Some even maintain a list, which they read every day; setting forth all they are grateful for.

Unsuccessful people are critical of themselves. They are often their own worst critics. They engage in negative, destructive thinking. They allow bad thoughts to enter their minds and take root, which eventually causes bad behavior. They lack motivation, enthusiasm, and often fall into states of mental depression that can last for days or weeks at a time. They watch too much negative programming on television and radio. They buy newspapers with headlines designed to stir base emotions. They frequent negative Internet sites. They feel hopeless and powerless.

One of the most successful techniques used to alter your mindset is to employ positive affirmations. These are words we can feed our minds every day to foster the attitude we desire. They need to be worded in such a way as if the trait you desire is already yours.

Positive Affirmations

"I complete my 'to-do' list every day."
"I accomplish my goals."
"I am lucky."
"I am successful."
"I make three hundred thousand dollars a year."

"I own a vacation home in Long Beach Island."

"I am a senior executive in my company."

"I pay for my child's college tuition out of my earnings or savings."

"I love my job."

"I love working with others."

"I am confident."

"I have a large network of relationships."

"I call my parents every week."

"I am a certified public accountant."

"I live my life in moderation."

Positive affirmations represent the picture of the individual you hope to be, the things you hope to achieve, assets you hope to own, and income you hope to earn. They must be specific and in the present tense to be effective. Make a list of positive affirmations and keep them by your side. Review them once in the morning, once in the afternoon, and right before you go to sleep. Let these positive affirmations seep into your mind every day. They represent your most positive, good thoughts, and they will take root. Events and circumstances will begin to manifest themselves around your positive thinking and opportunities will appear seemingly out of thin air.

Summary:

Successful people engage in Rich Thinking every day.

Rich Habit Promise Number Nine:

I will save ten percent of my gross income every paycheck.

Successful people pay themselves first. Before any bills get paid, successful people set aside ten percent of their gross earnings into some savings, investment, or retirement vehicle. They invest their money wisely, watch over their savings regularly, and set realistic goals for their investment returns. They have high credit scores, know their net worth, and monitor their personal balance sheet. They use only the most qualified financial professionals to maximize their returns and minimize their taxes. Every successful person employs the services of a certified public accountant, considered by many to be the most trusted financial advisor. They may also seek out attorneys or certified financial planners who specialize in financial or estate planning. They use these professionals to help them manage their money and their taxes.

Successful people have a retirement plan. They participate to the fullest extent permitted in retirement plans offered by their employers. Many of these retirement plans allow employees to put away, in a tax-deferred manner, ten percent or more of their earnings each year. If their company does not have a retirement plan, they create their own retirement plan by funding individual retirement accounts. They add to these accounts with every paycheck. They have retirement goals. They monitor their retirement plan regularly and make course corrections in an effort to reach their retirement goal.

Unsuccessful people pay themselves last. They live paycheck to paycheck, spending every penny to support their lifestyle. They are poor savers and carry excessive amounts of debt. They have home equity loans, which are tapped out. Their credit cards are maxed out, and they can barely make the monthly minimum payments. They have poor credit scores. They do not manage or monitor their credit scores. Unsuccessful people do not participate regularly in employer retirement plans or fund their own retirement plan. Some gamble excessively and view the lottery as their retirement plan. They take risks, which are either unnecessary or not thought through. They don't set aside ten percent of their earnings and, consequently, when they reach retirement age, they do not have enough retirement savings to allow them to retire with financial security. They rationalize that they cannot afford to set aside ten percent of their earnings. They are unwilling to alter their lifestyle in order to save adequately. More often than not, unsuccessful people have no choice but to continue working well into their retirement years.

Summary:

Successful people pay themselves first by putting ten percent of their paychecks into savings or retirement plans.

Rich Habit Promise Number Ten:

I will control my thoughts and emotions each and every day.

Successful people are the masters of their thoughts and emotions. They do not fall prey to anger, jealousy, excitability, sadness, or other petty emotions. They cast out all bad thoughts and emotions. They do not allow them even a second of life. They understand that bad thoughts create bad decisions that result in bad consequences. They replace these bad thoughts and emotions with good thoughts and positive emotions. They use the following technique when faced with a difficult situation that presents itself: "Think, Evaluate, and React." Thinking gives them time to understand the situation. Evaluating the situation buys more time to determine the correct course of action. Reacting is the last thing they do and most likely will be the appropriate reaction, as they took the time to choose their reaction.

Successful people are too busy to allow themselves to indulge in being sad or depressed. They engage in productive activities, which take their minds off their sadness or depression. They are constantly engaged in projects or self-improvement activities that promote positive feelings about themselves. Successful people feel as if they have total control over their emotions and thoughts.

Unsuccessful people fall prey to petty emotions. They let their emotions rule their behavior. They become easily depressed and feel as if they have no control over their lives. They react before thinking. They have adopted the bad habit of "Ready, Fire, Aim." As a consequence of this, there are many unsuccessful people sitting in prisons throughout the world.

Bad habits cause bad behavior, which results in bad decisions and ultimately a bad life. Bad thoughts occur when your mind is idle and not engaged in some constructive activity. You need to constantly be engaged in constructive activities, such as self-improvement, a worthwhile project, or a goal you want to accomplish. If you have a bad thought, immediately cast the bad thought out and refocus on the self-improvement activity, the constructive project, or the goal you wish to accomplish.

Summary:

Successful people are the masters of their thoughts and emotions.

Summary of the Rich Habits Promises:

1. *I WILL* form good daily habits and follow these good daily habits each and every day.
2. *I WILL* set goals for each day, for each month, for each year and for the long-term; *I WILL* focus on my goals each and every day.
3. *I WILL* engage in self-improvement each and every day.
4. *I WILL* devote part of each and every day in caring for my health.
5. *I WILL* devote part of each and every day to forming lifelong relationships.
6. *I WILL* live each and every day in a state of moderation.
7. *I WILL* accomplish my daily tasks each and every day; I will adopt a "DO IT NOW" mindset.
8. *I WILL* engage in rich thinking each and every day.
9. *I WILL* save ten percent of my gross income every paycheck.
10. *I WILL* control my thoughts and emotions each and every day.

Rich Habits at Work
– The Client

When they turned the last page of the Rich Habits Training Program, the client lifted his head to see his accountant, J.C. Jobs, staring at him, a slight smile drawing up the corners of his lips. "Well?" he asked.

"That's a lot of information."

"It is," J.C. replied, the smile spreading to his eyes and flushing his cheeks. "I want you to take the material home with you and think about the Rich Habits tonight. First thing tomorrow morning I want you to pull out the material and begin following the program. Review the Rich Habits in the afternoon and again just before you go to bed. Do this for the next thirty days. Follow the program, review the Habits, live the Habits, for the next thirty days." J.C. jotted down a date and time on the back of his business card and slid the card across the desk to his client. "I'll see you in thirty days."

The client woke early the next morning, eyes still cloudy from an early rise he was not yet accustomed to, and opened up the Rich Habits Training Program binder created for him by J.C. Jobs. "Let's see," he said to himself. "Rich Habits Number One requires me to list all of my bad habits in one column." The client did just as instructed. One by one he began to list all of his bad habits..

"I had no idea how many bad habits I had," he murmured to himself. As instructed by J.C. and the program materials, he began to invert his bad habits, one by one, turning them inside out.

	Bad Habits	Good Habits
1	I gamble on sports too much.	I did not gamble on sports today.
2	I smoke cigarettes.	I did not smoke a cigarette today.
3	I go out to restaurants too much.	I go to restaurants once a week.
4	I get to work late too often.	I get to work on time every day.
5	I get up late in the morning.	I wake up at 5 a.m. every day.
6	I don't pay enough attention to my wife.	I take a walk with my wife every day.
7	I eat too much junk food.	I did not eat junk food today.
8	I curse too much.	I did not curse today.
9	I spend too much time at the bar.	I did not go to the bar today.
10	I watch too much television.	I watched television for thirty minutes today.

These became his new good habits, which he followed diligently every day. This was not an easy task, but he desperately wanted to change his life, so follow them he did.

The client began to notice subtle changes in his life almost immediately. The gambling, he learned, was not only draining his bank account but was also taking time away from his wife and his business. He found that once he eliminated his gambling he no longer spent time at night during the week in the local sports bar, watching the teams he bet on. This meant he did not have to struggle as much to get up in the mornings. He found himself able to get to work much earlier than ever before, even after completing his Rich Habits morning ritual. The extra morning time in the office allowed him to get more things completed, allowing him to finish his workday with less stress and at a reasonable hour and giving him more quality time at home with his wife. His relationship with his wife began to perk up. She liked having him around and spending time with him. His business slowly began to improve. He wasn't pulling money out of his company bank account to finance his gambling. His company expenses seemed much more manageable.

His next task, Rich Habits Number Two, was to set daily, current year, next year and long-term goals. He had never set goals before, so this was entirely new to him. At first, his daily goals were hard to accomplish, but he adopted the "Do It Now" mindset required by Rich Habit Number Seven and after a few days he got the hang of this. He even began to look forward to ticking each daily goal off his list during the day. His annual goals, which he initially viewed as unrealistic, he now considered possible. His confidence grew each day. He felt productive and proud. He was imbued with a new thinking that he would and could eventually reach most of his goals. He became enthusiastic about his work, which fostered a desire to work even harder. His sales increased, as new opportunities opened up to his company.

Rich Habit Number Four required that the client devote part of each and every day in caring for his health. Exercise was something he had engaged in only sporadically and as a result he had never been able to lose weight. He guessed he was about twenty-five pounds overweight. Worse than his excess weight were his poor eating habits. As he had previously not been home much, opting for the local sports bar instead, he infrequently ate home-cooked meals. Most of his diet consisted of buffalo wings, burgers, French fries, and beer. To remedy this, each night, he and his wife walked an hour together after dinner. They both began to lose weight. As they became more motivated to lose weight, they began watching what they ate. Furthermore, the time they spent walking enhanced their relationship.

One by one he incorporated the Rich Habits into his life. And day by day his life changed for the better. All of the pieces to the puzzle of his life began falling into place. The client knew he was on the right track and everything was different now.

As the day of their follow-up meeting approached the client could barely contain his excitement. He had done just as J.C. had advised. He lived the Rich Habits for thirty days. This day he felt different, almost reborn, and he knew in his heart that he was on the path to personal and financial success.

The client shared with J.C. all of the things he was doing and the changes that had "miraculously" taken place during this thirty-day period. J.C. grew excited. His Rich Habits actually worked on someone other than himself! He could see that his client was now infused with the Rich Habits mindset. The transformation was complete. J.C. was very happy.

"Thank you so much," his client gushed as their meeting drew to a close.

"I want you to do me one favor," J.C. said, glancing down at the photo of Denise on his desk. The picture was from a vacation they had taken to Myrtle Beach the year before she passed away. She was bathed in sunlight and smiling from ear to ear. "When you come across another person in a financial situation similar to the one you are coming out of, I want you to reach out to help them by sending them to me. I will do for them what I have done for you."

"How similar?" the client asked. "There are a lot of people out there struggling."

"Ninety-five percent," J.C. added. He paused and considered the client's question for a moment. "You will know when their story stirs something inside you. When their story brings back strong memories of your difficulties. You will know when you look at the distressed individual and you feel as if you are looking in a mirror of your old life. When you come across that person, I want you to refer them to me. Will you do that for me?"

The client agreed and shook J.C.'s hand vigorously.

As the client exited his office, J.C. looked upon the picture of Denise on his desk and spoke to her, "As long as I'm alive I will do my best to help others become financially successful, Denise, so they may never have to carry the burden I carry with me every day. I love you, Denise, and once again, I'm sorry." Two tears streamed down J.C's cheeks – one representing regret and the other, hope.

Rich Habits at Work
– The Secretary

Dee took a seat on the left side of the room and cautiously eyed the others sitting around her. Small cardboard name cards sat in front of each person in the room. Nearby was a balding, slightly overweight man named Pheonix. In the right hand corner of the room sat a very well-dressed man in his mid-forties named Herb. He did not look as though he belonged here, but Dee figured that failure probably came in all packages. Others began to make their way into the large training room, finding their seats with their name cards. The other attendees were looking around, too. Everyone seemed nervous, timid. Dee considered that last thought. It wasn't that they were nervous or timid; they were beaten down, she decided. "No egos in this room," she said to herself. "We're all in the same boat," the voice in her head told her. "The S.S. Titanic." She laughed to herself at that one.

The training program lasted three hours. The instructor, a former financial mess turned Rich Habits devotee, enthusiastically expounded on each one of the Rich Habits. His enthusiasm infected everyone in the class. Individuals hardened by failure were laughing, high-fiving each other and sharing intimate details about their specific circumstances.

J.C. stopped in halfway through the training session and gave everyone a pep talk. As if that was needed. The entire day was all so uplifting. Dee, along with a hundred others just like her, cheered and backslapped each other on as they exited the room, program binders in hand. For that moment none of them felt like a failure.

Dee turned out to be one of J.C. Job's most enthusiastic students. Rich Habit Number One required Dee to list her bad daily habits. She attacked every one like a pouncing tiger. All told, Dee identified about ten bad daily habits she knew were holding her back. As instructed by the training material, Dee inverted every one of these bad daily habits and they became her new good daily habits.

Rich Habit Number Four instructed Dee to care for her health every day. She had never exercised or watched what she ate. As a result, Dee was unhealthy and close to obese. She decided to limit her consumption of food to 1,800 calories per day and do a minimum of thirty minutes of aerobics every day. Dee liked to eat, and in the early days of moderating her consumption of food she felt like she was starving herself. But the hunger pains soon began to fade. Dee was too heavy to jog, so walking was her best option. By the end of the thirty days Dee was walking or slowly jogging forty-five minutes each day. Her weight loss that first thirty days was an astonishing twenty-five pounds. "I have not weighed this much since I graduated high school," she proudly said to herself.

Rich Habit Number Five instructed Dee to examine all of her relationships and eliminate the relationships that were destructive. She knew her recent job loss was caused by the frequent "dire" emergencies heaped upon her by her family. These distractions were her eventual undoing at her old job. As a teenager, Dee's parents had abandoned her and she was left to the care of an unwilling aunt. Her aunt and cousins considered Dee a burden on them and they made no bones about this to Dee. Consequently, Dee carried a tremendous guilt for receiving assistance from them. This guilt continued into her young adult years and her aunt and cousins used this guilt to finagle Dee into bailing them out of financial emergencies. The relationship was a one-way street for Dee. They took, and took, and took from her. Never giving back. She decided that when she got back on her feet, she would not allow herself to be used by them ever again.

One Rich Habit at a time she began to reinvent herself.

Feeling confident one day, Dee reached out to her old boss, John Andrews. She wanted her job and her kind old boss back. Somehow Dee talked him into meeting her for lunch. At lunch Dee told John about the Rich Habits Training Program she was going through. John was impressed. He could see the effectiveness of the training in her obvious weight loss. Dee told John she had pulled away from her manipulating cousins and that she was not going to allow herself to be distracted that way by anyone or anything ever again. She told him she was confident she would be able to meet John's often-articulated, high expectations for her. John agreed to take Dee back for "one more try," as he put it.

Despite Nina's initial objections at her return to the company, Dee and Nina soon became fast friends. Nina, who ran most of the operations, found herself delegating more and more of her responsibilities to Dee.

Some years later, Nina took over as CEO of Sunblade and Dee took over Nina's operational responsibilities. Dee, with J.C. Job's enthusiastic support, took it upon herself to conduct Rich Habits training sessions for all Sunblade employees. The Rich Habits "fever" gripped the entire organization. John eventually sold his interest in Sunblade to Nina, Dee, and some of the other key employees, who all worked very hard to grow the company to a much bigger enterprise than the one John left them, making everyone, financially, very well off. Perhaps the most important thing to come out of Dee's Rich Habits transformation was her fight to gain control over her weight and health. At forty-four years of age, Dee can proudly look in her mirror at a lean and healthy reflection. To memorialize her second chance at life, thanks to the Rich Habits, Dee runs the Philadelphia half-marathon every year. This year Dee will run her twentieth half-marathon.

Rich Habits at Work
– The Car Dealer

Herb may have been one of the most functional of all of the Rich Habits students in his training class. His deficiencies were not many. But the few he had were devastating to his financial life. The one Rich Habit he realized he was violating every day was Rich Habit Number Five: I will devote each and every day to forming lifelong relationships. Herb had always viewed the customer as a one-time sale. He never took the time to build any relationships with the customers in his sales career. His attitude towards the customer, exhibited by his cut-throat selling skills, while very effective as an employee, became a cancer to his organization. It trickled down to the service department, the finance and insurance department, and to the sales department, creating a culture that kept away former customers. As a consequence, the dealership was forced to chase new customers every day. The old ones simply never came back to buy cars. Worse, they rarely frequented the service department, a major source of revenue in any car dealership. Herb committed to changing his dealership's culture to a more customer-friendly one.

The first thing Herb did was to put up a large sign in front of his dealership "Under New Management." He wanted everyone within (staff) and without (customers) his dealership to share the perception that things had changed at the dealership. Next, he reached out to his old boss, the one he had fought with many times over his treatment of customers. He confided in his old boss about the Rich Habits Training he was undergoing. His old boss was interested in helping Herb and agreed to meet with him twice a week to help educate him on successful customer relationship management techniques. He also introduced Herb to some valuable banking relationships that enabled him to refinance his existing debt and secure an extension on his floor plan financing. This bought Herb the time he needed to retrain his staff and allow for the change in the dealership's culture to take effect.

In time Herb's business improved. He had learned to treat his customers like gold. He was able to pay off his debts to the bankers and eventually no longer required floor plan financing as he could self-finance his inventory. He bought a second dealership some years later, and then a third, and a fourth, and so on, as the years passed by.

Today Herb is not only one of the largest automobile dealers in New England, he is also one of the top instructors at J.C. Job's Rich Habits Foundation, a non-profit organization established by J.C. to offer free Rich Habits training to those who do not have the financial means to afford the cost of attendance. Herb considers his proudest accomplishment the fact that he has trained nearly ten thousand individuals in the Rich Habits.

Rich Habits at Work
– The Insurance Salesman

The day following his Rich Habits training, Phoenix got busy. He reviewed each one of the Rich Habits. The one that bothered him the most was Rich Habit Number Three: I will engage in self-improvement every day. For the longest time Phoenix had convinced himself that he hated his job and must have missed his calling in life, whatever that calling might be. As such, he never truly devoted himself to his work. This was evidenced by his distain for reading anything having to do with his profession. He rarely, if ever, read any of the life insurance industry trade periodicals he received each month. He knew this had to change. The Rich Habits had opened his eyes to this glaring deficiency in his professional life.

Phoenix committed that first morning to reading his technical material thirty minutes each day. In the first few days he really struggled with this commitment. The reading felt to him like pulling teeth. But as each day went by, the chore became a little easier. After a week he had modified his new daily habit from thirty minutes to forty-five minutes and added product material to his reading list. He began keeping a notebook on new facts or sales strategies that came from his reading. His notebook began to fill up. He tested some of the sales strategies and seemed to have some luck. His pipeline started to fill up with solid leads. His appointments nearly doubled, which he acknowledged to himself was not hard to accomplish given his previous lead conversion success. Nonetheless, he was proud of his achievement. The more he read, the more success he seemed to have scheduling appointments, and the new strategies he was testing out were increasing his closing rates.

Rich Habit Number Four states: I will devote part of each and every day in caring for my health. When Phoenix finished his morning reading, he slipped on a pair of running shoes and took a jog outside. He guessed he was nearly forty pounds overweight. Most of his weight was in his belly with the rest seeming to inflate his face. He was only able to jog a mile or so at first, but within two weeks he was jogging two miles without much trouble. Two miles increased to three miles and his weight began to fall off. The drop in weight prompted him to moderate his eating and to stop smoking. Seeing the weight fall off motivated him to push himself harder and eat less each day. It didn't take long for ten pounds to disappear from his frame. His wife and son noticed the weight loss and that boosted his ego.

At night Phoenix made cold calls from the phone book. He never liked doing that before. But now he added this to his Daily Goal/To-do list. He still hated the cold calling but he remained committed to making these calls every night. A few cold calls panned out. One created a referral opportunity that led to a large life case. In fact, that case turned out to be one of the largest in his career. Inspired, he pushed himself to make more cold calls each night. This routine took away from his patronage of the local pub. He couldn't do both and besides, all those beers, he reasoned, would interfere with his ongoing weight loss. When he was done with his evening cold calling he rewarded himself with a beer from his refrigerator at home. That soon became a ritual and he enjoyed that nightly beer more than any beer he ever had at the bar.

One day, toward the close of the month, Phoenix was called into the office of his supervisor. "What's going on?" his supervisor asked with a slight half-smile. Phoenix never liked being called into the boss's office. For him, that was never a good experience. He was nervous in his reply. "Well, a lot, I guess – doing some things differently this month."

"That's why I asked you in here," his boss replied. "I just received the preliminary flash report for this month. You're production numbers are up. Looks like you had one big case, but what interests me is not that case but the other smaller cases."

"How do you mean?" Phoenix was now studying the report with his boss.

"You've got about a dozen small cases here. The numbers aren't individually significant, but when added together, they're pretty good. What are you doing?"

Phoenix was initially reluctant to confide in his boss about the Rich Habits Program he was following every day. This was such a personal thing to Phoenix. But his boss seemed sincerely interested and his reluctance soon abandoned him. He gave his boss an overview of the experiment he was undertaking. His boss was impressed.

"That's great Phoenix. I think you're onto something." His boss opened his draw and handed him an envelope.

"What's this?" Phoenix asked, looking at an envelope with his name on it. The envelope looked like a paycheck envelope to him.

"Open it up," his boss urged, a smile drawing up the corners of his lips.

Phoenix opened the envelope and to his surprise there was a check for one thousand dollars made out to his name.

"What's this for?" he asked in disbelief. He had never received any check before from his boss other than his meager paycheck.

"You came in third this month in production numbers. Third qualifies you for a monthly production bonus."

Phoenix's facial expression advertised his shock. His boss grabbed his hand, pulled it to him and shook it vigorously.

That night Phoenix showed his wife the check. "I feel like framing this," he told his wife. "I never got one of these before."

His wife hugged him and said, "Let's celebrate. Let's go out to dinner."

Phoenix held that thought in his head for a moment, then replied. "No. I can't. I've got to make some phone calls tonight. Let's celebrate Friday instead. Is that okay?"

"Sure. That's fine. We'll celebrate Friday."

The monthly production bonus became a recurring event for Phoenix. In time, that check grew larger as he moved from third to second, and then to number one. He liked being number one so much that he worked hard to stay number one for two years. After one of his most productive months, his boss asked Phoenix if he could train some of the others in the office in the Rich Habits. Phoenix approached J.C. Jobs who enthusiastically approved of the idea. The training decision turned out to be a wise one. In a short period of time, the firm's profit began to grow and grow as one producer after another increased their production numbers.

Phoenix was able to send his son to college and then graduate school. He gained control over his weight, spending, and savings. Phoenix continued to climb the company ladder, taking on more and more responsibility, and conducting Rich Habits training for all new hires.

The Commemoration of J.C. Jobs

The pews were filled, yet people continued to fill the church. Some stood three deep. When there was no more room inside the church, the crowd spilled out onto the church steps. The mass of mourners wound their way along the sidewalks in front of and across the church. The entire block was filled with people. The church bells rang loudly but could not drown out the chattering and sobs of the mourners. An altar boy scurried about outside with some wires and speakers so that those outside the church could participate in the ceremony inside.

"He saved my life," one of the onlookers could be heard saying to another above the din of the noise.

"Mine too," another chimed in.

Soon a chorus of "Me toos" reverberated outside the church.

An old man rose from his pew in the front of the altar and slowly made his way to the podium. He adjusted his glasses as he pulled out his notes, took a deep breath, and looked out upon the crowd or mourners, then down at his notes.

"Three-and-one-half-million people and growing every day. That is the number of people whose lives were transformed by J.C. Jobs and his Rich Habits followers. Most of these people have dramatically improved their lives. Before J.C. they were desperate, financially destitute, unhealthy, and emotionally broken. J.C. showed them the path to success. Their lives and the lives of their families, transformed forever. No one individual in recent times has helped so many people change their lives so dramatically. I know what I am talking about. I was J.C.'s guinea pig. A failing client who, in pleading desperation, asked, "What am I doing wrong? Forty-five years ago J.C. Jobs changed my life forever." The old man looked up from his notes to view the throng of people inside the church. They were all J.C.'s students or former students, he knew. "Each one of you owes your success in life to this great man."

He was not reading from his notes now.

"Each one of you was failing in life. No savings, no retirement funds, no college money, no assets, unhealthy, unhappy, and miserable at your lot in life. Your financial and emotional situation was an anchor around your neck, dragging you and your family down, until you were introduced to this giant of a man and his Rich Habits. Now you drive nice cars, have beautiful homes, vacation homes, retirement savings, more money than you will be able to spend in your lifetime. You're healthy, happy, and enthusiastic about life. The future of your children and their children is secure. They will never know of want. They will never know of need. They will never have to ask, 'What am I doing wrong?'"

The old man reached down for his notes, turned, made the sign of the cross, and walked from the podium directly to the casket that contained the body of J.C. Jobs. He put both hands on the casket, bent over slightly and kissed it gently. The crowd of people spontaneously rose from their pews and, one by one, lined up to kiss the casket of J.C. Jobs.